CAREERS IN THE
BUILDING TRADES

Construction & Building Inspector

Careers in the Building Trades

A Growing Demand

- Apprenticeships
- Carpenter
- Construction & Building Inspector
- Electrician
- Flooring Installer
- Heating and Cooling Technician
- Masonry Worker
- Plumber
- Roofer
- Working in Green Construction

CAREERS IN THE
BUILDING TRADES

A GROWING DEMAND

Construction &
Building Inspector

Andrew Morkes

MASON CREST

Mason Crest
450 Parkway Drive, Suite D
Broomall, Pennsylvania 19008
(866) MCP-BOOK (toll-free)
www.masoncrest.com

First printing

9 8 7 6 5 4 3 2 1

ISBN (hardback) 978-1-4222-4113-4
ISBN (series) 978-1-4222-4110-3
ISBN (ebook) 978-1-4222-7683-9

Cataloging-in-Publication Data on file with the Library of Congress

NATIONAL
HIGHLIGHTS

Developed and Produced by National Highlights Inc.
Proofreader: Mika Jin
Interior and cover design: Yolanda Van Cooten
Production: Michelle Luke

CONTENTS

INTRODUCTION:
The Trades: Great Careers, Good Money, and Other Rewards.......... 6
CHAPTER 1: What Do Construction and Building Inspectors Do?... 11
CHAPTER 2: Tools of the Trade 24
CHAPTER 3: Terms of the Trade 26
CHAPTER 4: Preparing for the Field and Making a Living 31
ON THE JOB: Interview with a Professional 44
CHAPTER 5: Key Skills and Methods of Exploration 49
CHAPTER 6: The Future of the Construction and Building
                            Inspection Occupation 63
Series Glossary of Key Terms 72
Index 75
Further Reading, Internet Resources and Video Credits 79

KEY ICONS TO LOOK FOR:

Words to understand: These words with their easy-to-understand definitions will increase the reader's understanding of the text while building vocabulary skills.

Sidebars: This boxed material within the main text allows readers to build knowledge, gain insights, explore possibilities, and broaden their perspectives by weaving together additional information to provide realistic and holistic perspectives.

Educational Videos: Readers can view videos by scanning our QR codes, providing them with additional educational content to supplement the text. Examples include news coverage, moments in history, speeches, iconic sports moments and much more!

Text-dependent questions: These questions send the reader back to the text for more careful attention to the evidence presented there.

Research projects: Readers are pointed toward areas of further inquiry connected to each chapter. Suggestions are provided for projects that encourage deeper research and analysis.

Series glossary of key terms: This back-of-the-book glossary contains terminology used throughout this series. Words found here increase the reader's ability to read and comprehend higher-level books and articles in this field.

INTRODUCTION

The Trades: Great Careers, Good Money, and Other Rewards

Trades workers play a major role in the success of economies throughout the world. They build structures ranging from houses to skyscrapers, keep the power on, and install and repair pipes that carry water, fuel, and other liquids to, from, and within businesses, factories, and homes, among many other job duties. Others inspect plumbing and electrical systems, roofs, and entire buildings to ensure that they comply with building codes and are safe for users. Yet despite their pivotal role in our society, only 6 percent of students consider a career in the trades, according to ExploretheTrades.org. Why? Because many young people have misconceptions about the trades. They have been told that the trades are low paying, lack job security, and other untruths. In fact, working in the trades is one of the best career choices you can make. The following paragraphs provide more information on why a career in the trades is a good idea.

Good pay. Contrary to public perception, skilled trades workers earn salaries that place them firmly in the middle class. For example, average yearly salaries for construction and building inspectors in the United States are $61,250, according to the U.S. Department of Labor. This salary is higher than the average earnings for some careers that require a bachelor's or graduate degree—including archivists ($54,570), event planners ($52,020), social workers ($50,710), recreational therapists ($48,190), and mental health counselors ($46,050). Construction and building inspectors who become managers or who launch their own businesses can have earnings that range from $50,000 to $200,000.

Strong employment prospects. There are shortages of trades workers throughout the world, according to the human resource consulting firm ManpowerGroup. In fact, trades workers are the most in-demand occupational field in the Americas, Europe, the Middle East, and Africa. They ranked fourth in the Asia-Pacific region. Construction inspectors are in especially strong demand in Canada and Russia, according to the recruitment firm Michael Page.

Provides a comfortable life without a bachelor's or graduate degree. For decades in the United States and other countries, there has been an emphasis on earning a four-year college degree as the key to life success. But studies show that only 35 percent of future jobs in the U.S. will require a four-year degree or higher. With college tuition continuing to increase and the chances of landing a good job out of college decreasing, a growing number of people are entering apprenticeship or community college programs to prepare for careers in the trades. And unlike college students, apprentices receive a salary while learning, and they don't have to pay off loans after they complete their educations. It's a good feeling to start your career without $50,000 to $200,000 in college loans.

Rewarding work environment and many career options. A career in the trades is fulfilling because you get to use both your hands and your head to solve problems and make the world a better place. Construction and building inspectors can work at construction sites, in the homes of clients, and in other settings. Many construction and building inspectors launch their own businesses.

Jobs can't be offshored. Trades careers involve hands-on work that requires the worker to be on-site to do his or her job. Construction and building inspectors need to be on-site to make sure that wiring is up to code, that blueprints have been followed, and that there are no dangers to a building's occupants. As a result, there is no chance that your position will be offshored to a foreign country. In an uncertain employment atmosphere, that's encouraging news.

Job opportunities are available throughout the United States and the world. There is a need for trades workers in small towns and big cities. If demand for their skills is not strong in their area, they can move to other cities, states, or countries where demand is higher.

Are the Trades Right for Me?

Test your interest in the trades. How many of these statements do you agree with?

☐ My favorite class in school is shop.

☐ I like to build and fix things.

☐ I like to use power and hand tools.

☐ I like projects that allow me to work with my hands.

☐ I enjoy observing work at construction sites.

☐ I like doing household repairs.

☐ I am interested in building structure and design.

☐ I like to watch home-repair shows on TV and the internet.

☐ I like solving problems.

☐ I like to figure out how things work.

If many of the statements above describe you, then you should consider a career in the trades. But you don't need to select a career right now. Check out this book on a career as a construction and building inspector and other books in the series to learn more about occupational paths in the trades. Good luck with your career exploration!

■ *An inspector notes the quality of the thermal insulation on a house that is under construction.*

Words to Understand

blueprints: A reproduction of a technical plan for the construction of a home or other structure. Blueprints are created by licensed architects.

building codes: Rules established by local, state, regional, and national governments that ensure safe construction. The National Electrical Code, which was developed by the National Fire Protection Association, is an example of a building code in the United States.

infrastructure: In relation to the construction industry, the systems of a city, region, or nation such as communication, sewage, water, transportation, bridges, dams, and electric.

self-employed: Working for oneself as a small business owner, rather than for a corporation or other employer. Self-employed people must generate their own income and provide their own fringe benefits (such as health insurance).

CHAPTER 1

What Do Construction and Building Inspectors Do?

The world would be more dangerous without construction and building inspectors. Buildings, bridges, and dams would be at higher risk of being constructed poorly and collapsing. People would be more apt to get shocked by faultily constructed electrical systems. More pipes would leak, and more elevators would get stuck between floors. Construction and building inspectors are skilled trades professionals who inspect the work of electricians, carpenters, roofers, heating and cooling technicians, and other trades workers at construction sites (including new buildings, as well as road, bridge, and other infrastructure projects). They also inspect homes and condominiums to make sure that remodeling work has been done correctly, as well as to ensure they are in good shape if they are being sold.

■ *A construction inspector takes notes at a work site.*

Some construction and building inspectors operate their own businesses. Others work for inspection companies, government agencies, architectural firms, and civil engineering consulting firms. To learn their skills and obtain experience, aspiring construction and building inspectors earn certificates or associate degrees in construction inspection, civil engineering, or construction technology. Others complete short apprenticeships or receive informal on-the-job training from experienced inspectors. Many inspectors have previous experience working as electricians, carpenters, plumbers, or in other trades careers.

This is a good career for those who are experts in construction techniques, building materials, and **building codes**, like to identify and suggest solutions for problems, and want the opportunity to make a good living without earning a four-year degree.

■ *A city construction inspector discusses his career.*

Types of Inspectors

The job duties of inspectors vary depending on their employer and what types of structures or infrastructure they inspect, although an inspector who works in one sector can also work in other sectors if he or she has enough skill, training, and experience.

Construction Inspectors

Construction inspectors examine entire buildings, roads, bridges, dams, sewer and water systems, and other structures that are being built or repaired. They also inspect the individual systems—electrical, plumbing, heating/cooling, etc.—that exist in some of these structures. Construction inspectors are employed by government agencies, inspection companies, architectural firms, and civil engineering consulting firms. Every inspection is different, but most inspectors do the following:

- Review **blueprints** and building plans to ensure that they meet building codes, local ordinances, zoning regulations, and contract specifications

- Approve building plans that pass their review, and identify and suggest changes when there are problems with plans

- Once construction begins, periodically visit construction sites to ensure compliance, including making sure that building materials (concrete, stone, steel, conduit, etc.), tools, and equipment meet quality standards, and that safety rules are being followed (At large construction sites, an inspector is on hand full-time to monitor the project.)

■ *There is strong demand for home inspectors in the United States because the U.S. economy has bounced back after the Great Recession.*

■ *Construction sites can be busy, muddy, and sometimes dangerous.*

- Educate builders about the review process and building codes
- Use surveying instruments and other equipment to perform inspections
- Issue violation notices and stop-work orders to correct issues
- Maintain daily logs, including photographs and video taken during inspections
- Write reports that detail their findings
- When the project is complete, perform a final inspection to identify any issues that need to be addressed

Some construction inspectors specialize in examining electrical, plumbing, heating and cooling, refrigeration, and other systems. Here are a few other types of specialists:

Plan examiners study blueprints and other plans for a structure to ensure that they comply with building codes, environmental regulations, and engineering principles.

Structural inspectors examine steel framework, reinforcing steel mesh and rods, concrete forms, concrete, and pre-stressed concrete to make sure they meet specifications and building codes.

Public works inspectors examine government construction projects. Some may specialize in inspecting highways, bridges, sewage treatment facilities, dams, or other structures. Or they may specialize in distinct construction tasks such as inspecting asphalt paving, construction that involves the use of concrete, or dredging operations required for bridges and dams.

Why Get an Inspection?

- For public works projects, inspections are required by law. They ensure that taxpayer money is well spent and that structures are constructed according to building codes (keeping users and occupants safe).
- Home inspections help identify the need for major repairs or fraud by the seller.
- Home inspections give home buyers and home sellers confidence that they are buying or selling a home that is in good condition.
- If major issues are identified during an inspection, the home buyer can use the inspection report to negotiate a lower price for the property or request that repairs be completed before the sale is final.

Fire inspectors examine structures to ensure that their components meet fire codes.

Coatings inspectors examine the paint and other coatings on bridges, pipelines, and other structures.

Elevator inspectors examine elevators, moving sidewalks, escalators, ski lifts, amusement park rides, and other lifting and conveying devices.

Disaster inspectors are employed by government agencies to inspect homes, apartment buildings, and other structures that have been damaged by hurricanes, flooding, tornadoes, earthquakes, and other natural disasters. They assess and document the condition of the structure so that government disaster relief payments can be issued to property owners.

What Home Inspectors Examine

- The overall structural quality of the building
- Plumbing systems
- Electrical systems
- Heating, cooling, ventilation, and refrigeration systems
- Fire detection systems
- Roofs
- Exterior and interior walls
- Insulation
- Floors
- Windows
- Garages
- Attics
- Crawlspaces
- Building foundations
- Decks

■ A home inspector discusses how he performs home inspections.

Building Inspectors

Building inspectors examine homes, condominiums, townhomes, and other new or previously owned buildings. They are also known as *home inspectors.* Building inspectors work for home inspection companies and government agencies, or they have their own businesses. A home inspector can work in the following capacities:

- For prospective home buyers who want an assessment of the condition of a new or existing home that they are buying
- For homeowners who want an assessment of the condition of their home before selling it
- For a government agency that employs inspectors to approve work on large remodeling projects and to ensure that construction contractors are following building codes and zoning requirements

Typical duties for home inspectors include:

- Studying blueprints and project specifications (for new construction inspections) to ensure that the building and its systems have been constructed properly
- Visiting the inspection site and explaining the inspection process to interested parties
- Beginning the inspection, which may last from two to four hours or longer (depending on the size and type of building)
- Performing a visual inspection of the building from the foundation to the roof (including exterior walls)
- Performing a visual inspection of the interior of the building to assess the condition of mechanical systems, floors, interior walls, and other components
- Operating all the major appliances and the heating, cooling, electrical, and plumbing systems to ensure that they work correctly
- Offering tips and advice to potential or current homeowners on how to effectively operate and maintain their homes
- Pointing out issues that arise and detailing what must be done to fix them (and providing more detail later in their written reports)
- Taking detailed notes during the inspection

■ *Inspectors who earn a bachelor's degree in surveying can become surveyors. Above, a surveyor uses a theodolite at a road construction site.*

- Taking photos and video during the inspection to provide further documentation
- When the inspection is complete, reviewing their findings with the client, and then preparing a report off-site and presenting it to their client, often within twenty-four hours since many inspections are time-sensitive

Some home inspectors pursue additional education to offer specialized services. They conduct testing for radon, asbestos, lead, carbon monoxide, or termites (or other pests). Others specialize in inspecting well and septic systems, swimming pools, or spas. Some inspectors serve as expert witnesses in legal proceedings, testifying under oath about building and construction issues and their inspection findings.

Work Environments

Construction and building inspectors split their time between offices (reading blueprints, writing reports, etc.) and inspection sites. At construction sites, the work environment can be busy, dusty, and noisy. Construction inspectors typically work forty hours a week, Monday through Friday, but they occasionally need to work at night and on weekends when projects are on a tight deadline. Inspectors often work alone, but they may be part of an inspection team for large projects.

Home inspection sites are usually much quieter and calmer. Inspection services are offered seven days a week. Most inspectors work about forty hours a week. Some inspectors may work four days, ten hours each day, with the remaining three days off. Others may work every day of the week, with their work hours varying each day. Many inspectors perform inspections during the day, and then write their inspection reports in the evening. Inspectors usually work alone.

Construction and residential work sites can be dangerous. Inspectors can be injured by jutting nails, falls from ladders, electric shocks, falling debris, and other hazards. As a result, inspectors take safety precautions and wear protective gear such as hard hats.

Inspectors work in all types of weather. They may have to climb ladders to inspect roofs and heating and air-conditioning units on cold, windy days or during the hottest days of summer. They often have to squeeze into tight spaces between buildings or air-conditioner units or furnaces, or literally crawl through crawlspaces. They may work in buildings in which heating or air-conditioning systems have not yet been connected.

Disaster relief inspectors must respond quickly after disasters. They spend days, or even weeks, away from home. This can be stressful if they have families. A construction inspector may be called on-site at any time if an accident occurs.

Starting Your Own Inspection Business

About 8 percent of construction and building inspectors in the United States are **self-employed**, according to the U.S. Department of Labor. They provide inspection services to clients, but they operate their own businesses. An inspection business might just be a one-person company, or it may employ additional inspectors, office staff, and other support workers. Many inspection businesses provide services to residential customers. Other companies offer their services to construction companies, government agencies, and civil engineering firms.

There are many reasons why people like being business owners. You get to be your own boss, decide what type of customers you'll cater to, and choose what hours you'll work. If your business is successful, you'll also have the chance to earn much more money than the average inspector.

But being a business owner is also challenging. You'll need to do administrative tasks such as scheduling appointments and talking with customers about your services, preparing contracts, billing clients, and handling payroll. You'll need to advertise your business in the newspaper and on the internet and social media; by attending community events; by conducting presentations in real estate offices; and by developing relationships with referral sources such as real estate agent brokers, real estate lawyers, mortgage lenders, and title companies. Although owning a business can be time-consuming and stressful at times, many business owners report that they find their careers both personally and financially rewarding.

Advancement Opportunities

Construction and building inspectors who complete specialized education and training are qualified to work in many related fields. Here are a few popular options:

Civil engineers design roads, buildings, dams, bridges, water supply and sewage treatment systems, airports, tunnels, and other infrastructure projects and systems. They use their skills to help troubleshoot problems during construction. Civil engineers typically have at least a bachelor's degree in civil engineering or a related field.

Construction managers oversee every aspect of a construction project—from the various types of trades workers (electricians, plumbers, steelworkers, etc. that do the actual work), to managing budgets, to ordering supplies and equipment, to ensuring that the job site is safe for workers. They typically have a lot of experience in the construction industry and a bachelor's degree in construction management.

Surveyors use a variety of measuring equipment and technologies to determine property boundaries. They have a bachelor's degree in surveying, land surveying and mapping sciences, or a related field.

Architects use computer-aided design and drafting and building information modeling software to create the designs for houses and other structures. They have a minimum of a bachelor's degree in architecture, and many have a master's degree.

Workplace Safety

There are many ways that inspectors can be injured during the inspection process. In rare instances, inspectors have even died during inspections. The most common injuries to inspectors include:

■ *Inspectors wear hardhats, safety glasses, and other gear to stay safe on the job.*

- Internal injuries from falls from ladders, stairs, roofs, or the collapse of work areas
- Internal injuries caused by falling through a rotten or damaged roof, staircase, or floor
- Cuts from protruding nails or screws, or from other sharp or jagged objects
- Electrocution from improperly installed electrical outlets, fixtures, or systems
- Burns from hot pipes or other equipment
- Eye injuries caused by foreign objects entering their eyes at construction sites
- Exposure to hazardous chemicals, fumes, and substances; raw sewage; and other toxic or carcinogenic (known to cause cancer) substances
- Knee, leg, or other injuries caused by kneeling for long periods or slipping on wet or icy surfaces
- Bites from pets or rats, snakes, bats, bees, spiders, and other animals
- Hearing damage from loud noises from machinery and tools.

How to Stay Safe on the Job

Like any workers, construction and building inspectors must follow safety practices to avoid injury. Here are a few safety measures to follow if you work as an inspector:

- Wear protective gear such as heavy gloves, hardhat, coveralls, ear plugs, and steel-toed work shoes with non-slip soles

- Use a respirator when working in any areas where there is danger of exposure to hazardous chemicals, fumes, and substances; raw sewage; and other toxic or carcinogenic substances

- Be extremely careful on ladders or when working at heights or in areas with wet floors or steps

- Secure exterior ladders on windy days to ensure that you will not fall or be stranded atop a roof

- If working alone, always carry a cell phone to use during emergencies

- Discuss potential safety issues with clients before beginning an inspection

Text-Dependent Questions

1. What type of inspectors examine the work done on road, dam, and bridge construction projects?

2. What are some of the best aspects of a career as an inspection business owner?

3. What kinds of safety gear do inspectors use to protect themselves?

Research Project

Talk to a construction or building inspector about what it's like to own a business. Ask if you can job shadow him or her in the office and at job sites.

CHAPTER 2
Tools of the Trade

Measuring and Investigative Tools

awl: A sharp hand tool that is used to dig into wood or other building materials to check for rot or other types of deterioration.

carbon monoxide (CO) analyzer: A device that measures CO levels in a home or building. Carbon monoxide is a colorless, odorless, and tasteless gas that is created when water heaters, furnaces, and boilers operate inefficiently, need servicing, or are improperly vented. It is poisonous and can injure or kill people.

combustible gas detector: A device that quickly detects the presence of combustible gases (those that can catch fire easily) such as methane, propane, butane, ethanol, ammonia, and hydrogen.

flashlight: A device that generates light from battery or other power. Inspectors use high-powered flashlights often in their work—especially to get a better look at areas that are inaccessible or that have poor or no lighting.

infrared thermometer: A digital tool that allows inspectors to check the temperature of heating and cooling system registers in hard-to-reach places, such as under large, heavy furniture.

laser measure: A device that allows users to take distance measurements instantly.

level: A device that is used to establish a horizontal plane. It is comprised of a small glass tube that contains alcohol or a similar liquid and an air bubble.

moisture meter: A handheld device that can either find elevated moisture levels hidden behind tile, vinyl, or other building materials beneath shower and bathroom floors, or actually measure the elevated moisture levels by touching the material with two pins on the device. Some meters can perform both functions.

multi-meter: A digital device that inspectors use to check for electrical current at switches, wires, or outlets.

screwdriver: A manual or powered device that turns screws; it is used by inspectors to open electrical boxes, furnace and air-conditioner panels, and other mechanical equipment.

tape measure: A flexible ruler made up of fiber glass, a metal strip, cloth, or plastic.

thermal imaging scanner: A device used by home inspectors and others to identify basic electrical connection and load problems, find moisture intrusion, detect energy loss/missing insulation, and perform other functions.

Safety and Access Gear and Equipment

dust mask: A protective covering worn over the mouth and nose to reduce the inhalation of dust and other airborne pollutants.

electrical gloves: Gloves that are used primarily to protect wearers from electrical shock, but also from injury by sharp objects.

high-traction roof boots: Footwear that is specially designed to allow inspectors to walk on roofs without slipping.

ladder: A device that is made out of metal, wood, or other materials that is used to climb up or down.

ladder tie-offs: Straps that secure ladders to a roof or structure. They keep the ladder from being blown down by strong winds and prevent it from slipping away from the building as a person climbs it.

respirator: An artificial breathing device that protects the wearer from breathing dust, smoke, or other toxic substances.

safety glasses: Protective gear that shields the eyes of inspectors from injury by protruding nails, sharp edges, and wires, as well as from sparks given off by short circuits on electrical panels.

spectroscope: A telescoping device with a camera attachment that allows inspectors to take photographs of steep, slippery, or dangerous roofs from the ground.

Computer and Recording Technology

building information modeling software: A computer application that uses a 3D model-based process that helps construction, architecture, and engineering professionals to more efficiently plan, design, build, and manage buildings and infrastructure.

digital camera: A standard, but high-quality, camera that allows inspectors to take multiple photographs and often also record video during the inspection process.

infrared camera: A special camera that creates images using infrared radiation. Different colors correspond to different temperatures, allowing the inspector to identify areas of a building that are abnormally cold or hot.

office and customer management software: Computer applications that help users track finances and manage billing, schedule appointments, draft correspondence, and perform other tasks.

CHAPTER 3
Terms of the Trade

air-conditioner: A system or a machine that cools air and distributes it to a home or building.

allergen: Any substance such as mold, pollen, dust, and pet dander that is recognized by the immune system and causes an allergic reaction.

blueprints: A reproduction of a technical plan for the construction of a home or other structure. Blueprints are created by licensed architects.

buckling: The unwanted bending of a building material—such as flooring or a door frame—as a result of wear and tear, the pressure of heavy weight, or contact with a substance such as water.

building codes: A series of rules established by local, state, regional, and national governments that ensure safe construction. The National Standard Plumbing Code, which was developed by the Plumbing-Heating-Cooling Contractors Association, is an example of a building code in the United States.

carbon monoxide: A colorless, odorless, and tasteless gas that is created when fuels such as natural gas burn with insufficient air. It is poisonous and can injure or kill people if it leaks into a home from a malfunctioning furnace.

caulk: Waterproof filler and sealant that is used to fill spaces around windows and doors, shower stalls, and bathtubs, as well as joints that may exist between floors and fixtures. Deteriorating caulking can allow the intrusion of water and cause damage to floors, walls, and other building components.

corrosion: A chemical reaction that causes deterioration of metal, stone, or other materials.

crawlspace: A shallow space between the first floor of a building and the ground.

current: A measure of electrical flow. It is measured in amperes.

flashing: Sheet metal that is used to prevent the entry of water at wall and roof junctions and around chimneys.

foundation: In a construction project, the part of the structure that connects it to the ground and evenly distributes the weight of the structure.

furnace: A heating unit that works in cooperation with an air-conditioner or heat pump.

green construction: The planning, design, construction, and operation of structures in an environmentally responsible manner. Green construction stresses energy and water efficiency, the use of eco-friendly construction materials (when possible), indoor environmental quality, and the structure's overall effects on its site or the larger community. Also known as green building.

groundwater: Water from a subsurface water source. If a building's basement is not properly insulated, groundwater can get into the basement and cause damage to flooring and walls and create mold.

ice damming: The buildup of ice and water at the eaves (where the roof meets or overhangs the walls of a building) of a sloped roof. It is caused by inadequate attic insulation or ventilation and other factors.

insulation: Material such as fiber glass, foam, mineral wool, and cellulose that is placed in walls, ceilings, crawlspaces, basements, and other areas to reduce heat loss or heat gain.

load-bearing wall: A wall that is built out of concrete, cinder block, or brick that supports the weight of the building and conducts the weight to the foundation.

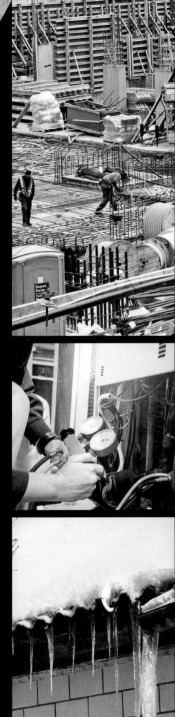

masonry: Construction using durable materials such as tile, brick, cement, stone (marble, granite, limestone, etc.), or similar materials.

pitch: In construction, the angle of rise in degrees from a horizontal starting point. The degree of pitch is an important consideration in staircase and roof construction because it affects the type of construction materials that are used, water drainage considerations, and the amount of room in the upper story or attic of a building.

plumb: Slang for a wall, post, beam, air-conditioner, furnace, or other structure that is perfectly vertical.

punch list: A list that details what needs to be done during a construction project or home rehab. Also known as a snag list.

recreational facilities: In the inspection industry, a phrase used to categorize swimming pools, spas, saunas, steam baths, and exercise, entertainment, athletic, playground, and other similar equipment.

roofing membrane: A layer or layers of waterproofing products that cover and move water from the roof.

settling: The lowering of a building or pavement due to heavy weight or shrinkage of building materials due to moisture content or other issues.

weather stripping: Material installed around windows and doors that is used to reduce the escape of heat or air conditioning.

■ *High school mathematics classes are highly recommended because inspectors use their math skills every day.*

Words to Understand

community college: A private or public two-year college that awards certificates and associate degrees.

fringe benefits: A payment or non-financial benefit that is given to a worker in addition to salary. These consist of cash bonuses for good work, paid vacations and sick days, and health and life insurance.

technical college: A public or private college that offers two- or four-year programs in practical subjects, such as the trades, information technology, applied sciences, agriculture, and engineering.

webinar: A class that is offered on the internet.

CHAPTER 4

Preparing for the Field and Making a Living

Educational Paths

There are many ways to train to become a construction and building inspector. Some people enter the field after earning just a high school diploma, but also having extensive experience as a carpenter, electrician, or other trades worker. Others earn certificates or associate degrees in building inspection technology, construction technology, engineering, or architecture from community colleges or technical colleges, or by participating in an apprenticeship program. Still others learn through informal methods such as working as an assistant to an experienced inspector, and taking classes and webinars offered by colleges and professional associations. You can be successful as an inspector by training in any of these ways. Regardless of how you prepare for the field, you'll have to study hard to get ahead.

■ *An apprentice (left) receives hands-on training from an inspector at a job site.*

High School Classes

High school classes provide good preparation for your college study, apprenticeship, or on-the-job training. In shop classes, you'll learn about construction concepts and safety practice; how to use hand and power tools; and how to build, troubleshoot, and fix things.

Some technical high schools offer specialized programs in plumbing, electronics, and other trades. In some programs, you can earn credits toward future completion of an apprenticeship program. Getting into one of these programs is a good idea if you plan to prepare to be an inspector by first working as an electrician or other type of trades worker or plan to go the inspector apprenticeship route.

■ *A trainee (right) receives on-the-job instruction from an experienced inspector.*

Mathematics classes (especially algebra and geometry) will give you the skills to determine if measurements are correct (such as if offsets and angles for piping meet code); assess numerical information on blueprints, building plans, and diagrams; and create job estimates, prepare invoices, manage budgets, and set payroll (if you own a contracting business). If you plan to start a business, you should also take accounting, business, marketing, English/writing, and computer science classes.

Foreign language classes are useful because you may work with clients and coworkers who do not speak English as a first language. It will be a lot easier to interact with others if you speak their language. And you'll get more business if you're multilingual (able to speak more than one language). Other recommended classes include science (especially chemistry), physics, and government.

Apprenticeships

Some people train to become construction inspectors by completing an apprenticeship program. An apprenticeship is a formal training program that combines classroom instruction and supervised practical experience. They typically last three to five years. Apprentices are paid a salary that increases as they obtain experience. A registered apprenticeship program is one that is approved by the U.S. Department of Labor. Similar programs exist in other countries. Program requirements for inspector apprenticeship programs vary by program and country. According to the California Apprenticeship Coordinators Association (in the United States), trainees complete a minimum of 1,500 hours of on-the-job training and 144 hours of related classroom instruction during each year of training in a four-year program.

In a construction inspection apprenticeship, you'll learn about:

- Blueprint and construction plan reading
- Reinforced concrete
- Structural steel and welding

The Pros and Cons of Inspector Training Paths

Technical School/Community College

Pros: Programs are shorter than apprenticeships—typically one to two years.

Cons: You must pay tuition and you do not get paid like apprentices do.

A Good Fit: For those who want to enter the workforce more quickly.

Apprenticeship

Pros: Provides a clear path to employment. You earn while you learn (unlike college), and your pay increases as you gain experience. College credit is available for some coursework. Credentials are respected by employers.

Con: Programs last three to five years.

A Good Fit: For those who like a structured environment that combines both classroom and hands-on training.

On-the-Job Training

Pros: Allows you to get to work right away and receive a salary.

Cons: Training might not be as detailed as an apprenticeship or degree program. Salaries are relatively low.

A Good Fit: For those who do not need a structured educational setting to learn, and who are able to pick up their skills and knowledge on the job.

- Prestressed and post-tension concrete
- Structural steel and bolting
- Structural masonry
- Soils testing
- Other specialized construction methods of testing and inspection

Entry requirements vary by program, but typical requirements include:

- Minimum age of eighteen
- High school education
- One year of high school algebra
- Qualifying score on an aptitude test
- No use of illegal drugs

Visit http://www.doleta.gov/OA/sainformation.cfm for information on apprenticeship training programs in the United States. If you live in another country, contact your nation's department of labor to learn more about training programs. Those who complete an apprenticeship are known as *journeymen inspectors*.

Technical and Community College

Many technical colleges and community colleges offer certificates and associate degrees in building inspection technology. Other aspiring inspectors earn credentials in engineering, architecture, general construction, or residential plans examination.

■ *Apprentices get to earn while they learn. Above, an apprentice inspector checks the quality of newly installed windows.*

Degree and certificate programs feature a combination of classwork, shop work, and hands-on experience via an internship or informal apprenticeship with a construction firm or government agency. Typical classes in a building inspection technology associate degree program include:

- Report Writing
- Oral Communication
- Industrial Chemistry
- Basic Building Inspection Techniques
- Building Codes and Ordinances
- Plumbing and Mechanical Inspection
- Electrical Inspection

■ *Networking is a great way to learn more about job opportunities.*

Did You Know?

Inspectors who are certified typically earn higher salaries and have better job opportunities than those who are not certified. Some U.S. states even require inspectors to have certain types of certifications to work in the field. Here are some popular certifications:

Association of Construction Inspectors: Certified Construction Inspector, Certified Construction Project Manager, Certified Construction Consultant

Canadian Association of Home and Property Inspectors: National Certificate Holder

International Association of Electrical Inspectors: Certified Electrical Inspector, National Certification Program Construction Code Inspector, Canadian Certified Electrical Inspector

International Association of Plumbing and Mechanical Officials: Various certifications in residential and commercial inspection, plumbing plans examination, and other areas

NAESA International: Qualified Elevator Inspector

National Fire Protection Association: Certified Fire Inspector, Certified Fire Plan Examiner, and many other credentials

- Administration of Building Regulations
- Plan Review
- Soils, Grading, and Waste Water Control
- Construction Blueprint Reading
- Inspection and Fire Prevention
- Strength of Materials
- Green Construction Techniques
- Energy Efficiency Construction Techniques

Salaries for Construction and Building Inspectors by U.S. State

Earnings for construction and building inspectors vary widely by state based on demand and other factors. Here are the five states where employers pay the highest average salary and the states in which employers pay the lowest salaries.

Highest Average Salaries:

- Alaska: $86,470
- California: $83,690
- Nevada: $74,660
- Washington: $73,340
- New Jersey: $67,480

Lowest Average Salaries:

- Montana: $44,190
- Arkansas: $46,090
- Indiana: $46,790
- Tennessee: $46,920
- South Dakota: $47,710

Source: U.S. Department of Labor

■ *Learn about classroom, web simulation, and hands-on inspection training offered by the American Home Inspectors Training Institute.*

On-the-Job Training

Another way to train to become an inspector is to work as an assistant to an experienced inspector in a home inspection business, at a construction inspection firm, or for other employers of inspectors. In this type of learning situation, you'll receive an entry-level salary and gradually build your skills and experience over the course of several years on the job. During this time, you add to your experience by taking classes at community or technical colleges or through professional inspection associations. Gradually, you'll gain enough experience to pursue licensing and/or certification as an inspector. At that point, you'll be asked to stay on at your company as an inspector, or you may decide to start your own business.

Getting a Job

There are many ways to get a job once you complete your training. You might get a job offer through your apprenticeship program or through your college's career services office, but if not, you'll have to look for a job. Here are some popular job-search strategies:

■ *Learn some networking do's and don'ts.*

Start Networking. The majority of all jobs are filled via networking. Someone you knew in school tells you about a job. A friend of a friend knows about an inspection company that's hiring. Someone you've talked to at a social networking site, whom you've never met, steers you to a job opportunity. You get the idea.

Networking may seem complicated, but it's really not. It's just a way to trade information with others who are seeking a job, and help each other. You have two types of networks: personal and professional. Your personal network consists of friends and family. Your professional network consists of the following types of people:

- Fellow apprentices and classmates
- Instructors
- Your family or friends who know people in the construction or home inspection industries
- People you meet at inspection industry events
- People you meet online, including at social networking sites such as LinkedIn

But this list is just a start. Tell everyone you're looking for a job, but be specific. Tell people what type of job you're seeking (construction industry, home inspection, government agency, private company), where you want to work (close to home, willing to move for the right position), and your educational background. This will save people time. Be sure to help out your classmates, fellow apprentices, and family and friends who are also looking for jobs.

Check Out Job Boards. Inspector jobs can be discovered by checking out internet job boards that allow users to search by job type, employer name, geographic region, salary, and other criteria. They are sponsored by inspection associations, government agencies, and social media sites. While you're obviously not ready to start looking for a job, viewing job listings can give you a better idea of the duties of inspectors and the educational requirements necessary to enter the field. Here are a few popular job boards:

- https://acia.com/job-board
- http://careers.iaei.org
- http://careercenter.iapmo.org
- https://www.glassdoor.com
- https://www.linkedin.com
- https://www.usajobs.gov (U.S. federal government job board)
- https://www.jobbank.gc.ca (Canadian federal government job board)

Join and Use the Resources of Unions and Professional Associations. A union is an organization that seeks to gain better wages, benefits, and working conditions for its members. They are also called *labor unions* and *trade unions*. About 14 percent of all construction workers (including construction inspectors) in the United States belong to a union. (Home inspectors typically do not belong to unions.) Some construction inspectors are members of the International Brotherhood of Teamsters and the International Union of Operating Engineers.

Professional associations are a key resource for inspectors. They offer membership, training opportunities, certification, career information, publications and blogs, and networking events. Most countries have at least one professional association for inspectors. For example, major organizations in the United States include the American Construction Inspectors Association, American Society of Home Inspectors, Association of Construction Inspectors, National Fire Protection Association, and Women in Code Enforcement and Development. Inspectors in Canada can join the

■ *Owners of inspection firms can earn $50,000 to $200,000 or more a year.*

Canadian Association of Home and Property Inspectors. International inspection associations include the International Association of Electrical Inspectors, International Association of Plumbing and Mechanical Officials, International Code Council, and NAESA International.

How Much Can I Earn?

The occupation of construction and building inspector is one of the highest-paying trade careers. They earn average salaries of $61,250 a year, according to the U.S. Department of Labor (USDL). The average salary for all construction workers is $48,900. This salary will make you a member of the middle class (a category that is based on what a person earns—typically 25 percent to 65 percent of household income) in many countries. Not bad for a career that doesn't require an expensive four-year degree.

Some inspectors train for the field via an apprenticeship. As an apprentice, you'll start out by earning between 30 percent and 50 percent of what an experienced inspector makes. The USDL reports that the average starting salary for all apprentices is $60,000.

Average Earnings by Employer

The USDL reports the following average yearly earnings for construction and building inspectors by type of employer:

- Federal government agencies, $71,930;
- Nonresidential building construction, $71,700;
- Architectural, engineering, and related firms, $61,990
- Local government agencies, $60,550;
- Management, scientific, and technical consulting services firms, $60,520;
- State government agencies, $56,590.

Top Earners

The top 10 percent of construction and building inspectors earn more than $94,000. You'll make the big bucks if you are very skilled at your job, manage other inspectors, or live in a big city or other area where there is a shortage of inspectors.

Owners of inspection companies can make $50,000 to $200,000 or more, depending on the size of their businesses.

If you work as a salaried employee, you'll receive **fringe benefits** such as medical insurance, a pension, and other benefits. If you own your firm, you'll have to provide your own benefits.

Text-Dependent Questions

1. What are some typical classes for those who prepare to become inspectors at a community or technical college?

2. What is a union?

3. How much money can inspection business owners earn?

Research Project

Talk to inspectors who trained for the field in different ways (apprenticeship, college, assistant to experienced inspector). Ask them the following questions: How long did the training take, and what did it involve? What did you like and dislike about this type of training? If given the chance, would you train the same way? What advice would you give to a young person regarding training to enter the field? Prepare a report that summarizes the interviews. Try to determine what would be the best training approach for you.

ON THE JOB
Interview with a Professional

Heidi Richards is the owner of H.R. Inspection Services (http://www.hrinspectionservices.com) in South Portland, Maine.

Q. How long have you worked as an inspector?

A. I have been inspecting properties since the mid 90s as an insurance adjuster. I started my home inspection business in November 2016.

Q. What inspired you to get into this field?

A. I have always been interested in construction and how properties are built. I enjoy learning about new construction materials that come on the market. In addition, I want to make sure that the home my clients are hoping to buy is exactly what they are getting—no "hidden surprises," so to speak.

Q. How did you prepare for this field?

A. I took an online course to obtain my home inspector certification. Maine is not a state that requires certification, but I feel it is extremely important because there are standards of practice to be followed.

Q. Can you please tell me about a day in your life on the job?

A. An inspection for me starts with the exterior. I start from the roof and work my way down to the foundation. On the inside of the home, I start inspecting the attic and work my way to the basement. In addition, I test the electrical outlets, checking the panel box for any faulty install and condition. I test the plumbing and heating to make sure these systems are working properly.

Q. What is the most rewarding part of your job?

A. The best part of my job is a satisfied client. It's rewarding when the client is aware of any issues with the home and is able to get those repairs taken care of by the seller or negotiated in the price. I enjoy giving my clients the knowledge they need to make the right decision for them.

Q. What kind of personal traits do you think are important for inspectors?

A. I think it's important for inspectors to be personable. They have to not only have the knowledge, but be able to communicate the information to their clients. It's not up to the inspector to give his or her opinion about a property, but instead simply state the facts of the condition of the property to allow his or her clients to make the right decision for them.

Q. What advice would you give to someone who is considering a career as an inspector?

A. Meet and try to job shadow an inspector who has been in the industry for some time. The best way to learn is hands-on with a great inspector who is more experienced and knowledgeable than you are. Ask real estate agents who they like to use for an inspector, and contact that person. Learn, learn, learn!

Reuben Saltzman is the co-owner and president of Structure Tech Home Inspections (http://structuretech1.com) in St. Louis Park, Minnesota. He is also the author of a blog (http://structuretech1.com/blog) about home inspections and home-related topics in the Minneapolis/ Saint Paul areas.

Q. How long have you worked as an inspector? What inspired you to get into this field?

A. I started training to be a home inspector at about six years old. My dad was a carpenter, and I got to go along with him and help him on the job a lot. I was homeschooled until fifth grade, so I ended up spending a lot of full days doing demolition and carpentry. Up until I was old enough to get my first real job at the age of sixteen, I spent my summers working with my dad doing carpentry.

When I got my first real job at a hardware store, I couldn't believe that I was getting paid to just stand there and cashier or stock shelves. It was the easiest job in the world—at least compared to carpentry. Every job I've ever had has been far less physically demanding than carpentry.

Getting back to the question, my real desire was always to be a teacher. All throughout junior high and high school, I wanted to be a teacher. I enjoy teaching others and I'm good at it. I always thought I'd grow up to be a teacher and, as it turns out, I was kind of right.

I graduated from high school in 1997, and my dad purchased Structure Tech that same year. He had been doing home inspections part-time for many years, but this purchase pushed him into full-time inspector status. I started with Structure Tech that year, answering the phone and writing reports. I worked full-time at first, then part-time, then a few hours a month while working full-time at Home Depot.

In 2004, my dad convinced me that I could satisfy my desire to teach by becoming a home inspector, and he was right. I've been a home inspector ever since.

Q. Can you tell me about a day in your life on the job?

A. These days, I spend most of my time managing Structure Tech. I don't do a whole lot of home inspections anymore—maybe one per week. For the rest of the inspectors in my company, however, their day begins with their morning commute. We typically perform two inspections per day, one in the morning and one in the evening. We arrive at our inspection about fifteen minutes before the scheduled time to help make sure that we're the first ones there.

We typically meet our clients right at the beginning of the inspection, and we encourage our clients to follow us around during the inspection. We explain how the house works, and we explain our findings as we go through the house. We eat lunch on the road in-between inspections, and if we're lucky, we type up a good portion of our morning report before the afternoon inspection. We do not type reports on-site; we find that doing so takes away from our time with our clients.

We then do an afternoon inspection. After that, we head home and type the reports. Most reports can be typed in one to two hours—but not all of them. Some take three to four hours. This can make for long days, but we charge accordingly for our services.

Q. What surprised you the most when you first became an inspector?

A. What surprised me most after becoming a home inspector were the fearful attitudes of so many other home inspectors. My dad taught me to inspect houses as thoroughly as possible, use the best tools available, walk roofs, crawl to the farthest reaches of attics—all that jazz. I learned that many home inspectors have quite the opposite attitude. Many inspectors feel that the more they do and the more tools that they use, the more likely they are to get sued. Many home inspectors are terrified of being sued. They use a strong contract and their Standard of Practice as a shield to protect themselves from lawsuits, rather than doing more thorough inspections. I know that this sounds crazy, but it's true.

Q. What is the most rewarding part of your job?

A. The most rewarding part of my job is finding those hidden defects that I think most other inspectors would not have found. I think of this as an Easter egg hunt. Most homes have hidden problems, and it's my job to find them. When I find defects, and especially defects that appear to have been covered up, I'm invigorated. I always feel justified in going the extra mile. That, and seeing online reviews come in for my employees, too. I take a lot of pride in seeing my employees succeed.

Q. What kind of personal traits do you think are important for inspectors?

A. Hands down, without a doubt, the most important personal trait for a home inspector is excellent communication skills. Our job is not to simply identify defects with a home; our job is to convey that information to our clients and explain the significance of these defects. We need to make a big deal about the big stuff and a little deal about the little stuff. If we inspect a house and give the same level of importance to everything, we're doing a huge disservice to our clients. This ability to communicate must come through in person and in our reports. This means that home inspectors must be personable, good at reading people, good listeners, and calm. We need to be able to tailor our messages to different types of clients, and this is all about being able to read people. Home inspectors should also have good spelling and grammar skills. A large portion of this job involves writing reports.

Q. What advice would you give to someone who is considering a career as an inspector?

A. For anyone who is considering a career in home inspection, I recommend first going along on some inspections with an experienced home inspector to get a better idea of what's involved. Next, you'll need to decide if you'd rather work for a home inspection company or you'd rather be self-employed. This profession has traditionally been dominated by one-man shops, but that dynamic is beginning to change. I believe that more women are entering this profession, and the number of multi-inspector companies is increasing.

For anyone interested in working for someone else, get in contact with some multi-inspector company owners and ask them questions. They probably get asked these questions a lot, and they'll probably have some well-thought-out answers. I get asked these questions so often that I've blogged about it: http://structuretech1.com/updated-home-inspector-training-advice.

For anyone looking to be a solo-operator, be aware that the technical training to become a home inspector will be the easiest part of the job—not to say it's easy. The hardest part will be running a business and generating business.

■ Inspectors must be extremely detail-oriented so that they don't miss any problems that could create issues for clients.

Words to Understand

photovoltaic: A type of technology that is used to generate electricity directly from sunlight via an electronic process.

rehab: In the construction industry, to restore or rehabilitate a structure, typically a home.

scaffold: A temporary raised structure that trades workers use to work at heights that would otherwise be hard to reach.

soft skills: Personal skills that people need to develop to interact well with others and be successful on the job. They include communication, work ethic, teamwork, decision making, positivity, time management, flexibility, problem-solving, critical thinking, conflict resolution, and other skills and traits.

CHAPTER 5

Key Skills and Methods of Exploration

What All Construction and Building Inspectors Need

There are many skills that go into being a successful construction or building inspector. Some involve using your critical-thinking abilities, while others involve writing and speaking well. Here are the most-important traits for construction and building inspectors:

Detective and analytical skills: A skilled inspector has an almost super-human ability to find problems and construction issues that the average person—or even the average inspector—misses. You will need

■ *Inspectors need excellent communication skills because they must be able to concisely explain their findings to construction managers and others.*

to be able to look at every home or construction site as a type of mystery that needs to be solved. You need to be able to identify what's right and not right (e.g., cracks in the foundation, wiring that's not up to code, etc.).

- **Detail-oriented:** You must be extremely attentive to detail because your work directly affects the health and safety of people.

- **Communication and customer-service skills.** You need to be able to explain—in everyday terminology—what is wrong and what needs to be done to fix the problem. When interacting with customers, you must be polite, courteous, friendly, and patient. You also need strong grammar, spelling, and writing skills in order to be able to craft detailed technical reports that explain what issues you found, and what needs to be done to fix them.

- **Time-management skills.** If you work as a home inspector, you'll need to work quickly, but carefully, to complete inspections within the expected time frame so that you can move on to the next inspection site. If you don't stay on schedule, you won't be able to earn enough money to make a living. Strong time-management skills are also needed because an inspection report is often needed quickly to help complete the real estate transaction or, in the instance of a construction project, keep the project on-schedule and on-budget.

■ *Inspectors must be able to work effectively on their own—managing their time and being able to handle any inspection issues that arise.*

Home Inspection Nightmares

Here are some of the worst issues discovered by home inspectors, according to the American Society of Home Inspectors and *This Old House:*

- A live snake and a very dead rat in a breaker box
- Vines growing down chimneys
- Icicles in the basement
- A shower head located by an electrical panel
- No circuit breakers in a circuit breaker box
- Twelve light switches in a row; only one worked
- A World War II mortar shell in an attic
- A glass jar used on a roof to keep the rain away from an exposed electrical wire entering a house
- A box of explosives, with a wire attached to it, in a crawl space
- A storage shed used as the only support for an outdoor staircase

- **The ability to successfully deal with conflict and stay cool under pressure.** Construction managers, homeowners, real estate agents, and others sometimes become angry or argumentative when they get bad news about major issues that need to be fixed. You must be able to calmly explain the facts behind your reports and deescalate potential arguments.

- **Self-knowledge and a willingness to continue to learn:** You need to know what you don't know—meaning that you are not overconfident and arrogant about your abilities. For example, if you are asked to examine a new **photovoltaic**-powered heating system, but have no knowledge of these systems, you should bring in an expert to do this aspect of the inspection. Building codes, construction materials and techniques, and inspection equipment and practices are constantly changing, so you need to take continuing education classes throughout your career to upgrade and expand your knowledge.

Did You Know?

Professional organizations can help you find a construction site tour. For example, the Construction Industry Training Board arranges tours of construction sites for young people in England, Scotland, and Wales. In a recent year, it organized 3,000 tours at more than 130 construction sites across the United Kingdom—so there are a lot of opportunities. In the United States, organizations such as Associated Construction Contractors of New Jersey organize tours. Contact construction associations in your area to see what's available.

- **Physical strength and good health.** You'll spend a lot of your work day stooping, bending, reaching, kneeling, and even crawling—often in tight spaces. You'll also occasionally need to climb ladders and scaffolds, so good balance is important.

- **Ability to use technology.** You'll need to know how to use digital and video cameras to record information during inspections, as well as present these resources in reports. In addition to basic cameras and video equipment, you need to know how to use combustible gas detectors, infrared thermometers, thermal imaging scanners, and other digital and electronic devices. If you plan to start your own inspection business, you need to be familiar with office management software and be skilled at using the internet and social media to promote your business and interact with customers.

- **Ability to work independently.** You should be able to follow instructions without supervision, work hard, and be a good time manager.

- **Honesty and strong ethics:** The best inspectors always tell the truth and never lie to gain an advantage over their clients. They never accept bribes (illegal gifts of money or other things that have value) to "overlook" faulty electrical wiring, hidden water damage, or other issues that can cause injuries, illness, or even death. Construction and building inspectors have gone to jail and had their careers ruined because they accepted bribes. Always be honest and don't be one of those people.

■ *View forty-seven home inspection issues in under three minutes.*

Exploring Construction and Building Inspection as a Student

There are many ways to explore this field and the construction industry in general. Here are some tips to learn more:

Take Some Classes. Your middle school or high school is a great place to begin building the skills and knowledge you'll need as an inspector. Start with shop classes. Many inspectors have backgrounds in carpentry, plumbing, and electrical work, so shop classes will give you a good introduction to these areas. You'll learn how to use hand and power tools and measuring devices (such as screwdrivers, hammers, saws, and levels), build and fix things, and follow good safety practices. Some technical high schools offer specialized programs in plumbing, welding, heating and air-conditioning repair, carpentry, and other trades.

If you plan to start your own inspection firm, business, accounting, finance, and marketing classes will be useful.

Psychology classes will teach you about human behavior, and philosophy and current events courses will help you to develop your critical-thinking skills.

Here are some other classes that will come in handy as you prepare for a career as an inspector:

- Mathematics
- Physics

- Chemistry
- English/writing
- Computer science

Watch Home-Improvement Shows. There are many shows on the internet, television, and cable that show tradespeople at work and the big picture of a building being **rehabbed** or built from scratch. These will provide an overview of construction techniques and the types of issues encountered by inspectors. Here are a few to check out:

- *This Old House:* http://www.pbs.org/show/old-house
- *Holmes on Homes:* http://www.hgtv.com/shows/holmes-on-homes
- Many shows on HGTV: http://www.hgtv.com/shows

■ *Job shadowing an inspector is a good way to learn more about the field.*

Job Shadow or Conduct an Information Interview with an Inspector. During a job shadowing experience, you'll follow an inspector around for a few hours or an entire day. You'll learn firsthand how to identify problems with homes or at construction sites (perhaps a roof that's not pitched correctly, concrete that has been improperly mixed, or hidden water damage that's creating high mold levels). You can ask inspectors questions about their work, try out an infrared thermometer, multi-meter, or other testing device, or simply soak in the work environment at a bridge or building construction site.

An information interview is just a conversation with a person in a particular field that allows you to learn more about a career. They can be conducted in-person or on the phone, and typically last from ten to twenty minutes. Here are some questions to ask during the interview:

- Why did you decide to enter this career?
- Can you tell me about a day in your life on the job?
- What's your work environment like?
- What do you do to keep yourself safe on the job?
- What are the most important personal and professional qualities for people in your career?
- What do you like best and least about your career?
- What is the future employment outlook for inspectors? How is the field changing?
- What can I do now to prepare for the field (classes, activities, projects, etc.)?
- What do you think is the best educational path to becoming an inspector?

Your shop teacher, school counselor, construction club teacher-mentor, and family or friends who have contacts in the construction or home inspection industries can help arrange information interviews and job shadowing experiences. Professional associations and unions can also help.

Join or Start a Construction Club at Your School. You won't find a home inspection club at your school, but you can join your school's construction club. In such a club, you'll learn about carpentry, plumbing, masonry, metalworking, and other construction specialties; use tools such as drills, hammers, and saws; and learn how to troubleshoot and repair mechanical devices. Some clubs even go out in their communities and help trades workers fix up homes for the elderly or homes that have been damaged by tornadoes or other natural disasters. Your faculty advisor may also be able to set up presentations by construction workers (including inspectors), tours of construction sites, or job shadowing experiences with home inspectors. If your school doesn't have a construction club, start one with your classmates!

Read About Construction and Building Inspection. Reading inspection industry blogs, reports, and journals is a good way to begin to familiarize yourself with industry lingo, common issues inspectors encounter during home and construction site inspections, and trends in the industry. Some of the terms and topics might seem confusing at first, but as you read more you'll start to understand the world of inspection. Check out Chapter 2: Tools of the Trade and Chapter 3: Terms of the Trade for additional help. Here are some popular publications and resources:

- *ASHI Reporter* (http://www.ashireporter.org). This publication from the American Society of Home Inspectors (ASHI) has all kinds of useful articles and photographs of common issues encountered by home inspectors.

- The ASHI Blog (http://www.homeinspector.org/Blog) features great stories, photos, and videos about home inspection topics.

- *IAEI News* (https://iaeimagazine.org/magazine), which is published by the International Association of Electrical Inspectors, offers stories about common challenges faced by electrical inspectors, new technology (such as photovoltaic systems), and much more.

Another good way to learn more is to read sample home inspection reports. Doing so will allow you to see the types of issues inspectors encounter on a typical day and how inspectors put a report together using both photos and text. The International Association of Certified Home Inspectors offers several sample home inspection reports at https://www.nachi.org/home-inspection-report-samples.htm.

Take a Virtual Tour. The American Society of Home Inspectors offers a Virtual Home Inspection Tour (http://www.homeinspector.org/Home-Inspection-Virtual-Tour). This neat tour allows you to learn how inspectors investigate various areas (roof, heating, interiors, etc.) of a home. You can also view photos of typical problem areas. The International Association of Certified Home Inspectors offers a variety of videos that explain the inspection process at https://www.nachi.org/tv. Finally, check out YouTube to view videos of home inspections.

■ *A home inspector discusses her work.*

■ *Touring a construction site is an excellent way to learn more about the work of inspectors and the construction industry in general.*

■ *A good way to learn more about trades careers is by participating in competitions. Above, a young man competes in a carpentry contest.*

Participate in a Competition. Competitions are sponsored by schools, local park districts, or regional, national, or international membership organizations for young people who are interested in the trades. These organizations don't offer contests in which you can demonstrate your knowledge of inspection techniques, but they do offer competitions in many trades specialties as well as in **soft skills**. Since many inspectors started out as trades workers, or simply have a lot of knowledge of carpentry, plumbing, and other trades areas, participating in these contests is a good idea. Here are two popular contests that will allow you to test your abilities against your classmates or students from around the country or world, develop your skills, and make new friends:

SkillsUSA (http://www.skillsusa.org) is a national membership organization that serves middle school, high school, and postsecondary students who are interested in pursuing careers in the trades and technical and skilled service occupations. Its

Sources of Additional Exploration

Contact the following organizations for more information on education and careers in construction and building inspection:

American Construction Inspectors Association
http://www.acia.com

American Society of Home Inspectors
http://www.homeinspector.org

Association of Construction Inspectors
http://www.aci-assoc.org

Canadian Association of Home and Property Inspectors
https://www.cahpi.ca

International Association of Electrical Inspectors
http://www.iaei.org

International Association of Plumbing and Mechanical Officials
http://www.iapmo.org

International Code Council
http://www.iccsafe.org

NAESA International
http://www.naesai.org

National Fire Protection Association
http://www.nfpa.org

Women in Code Enforcement and Development
http://www.wicedicc.org

SkillsUSA Championships involve competitions in one hundred events. Students first compete locally, with winners advancing to state and national levels. A small number of winners can even advance to compete against young people from more than seventy-five other countries at WorldSkills International, which was recently held in Abu Dhabi, United Arab Emirates, and in Leipzig, Germany. Competitions that will be of interest include:

- Building Maintenance
- Carpentry
- Customer Service
- Electrical Construction Wiring
- Electronics Technology
- Heating, Ventilation, Air Conditioning & Refrigeration
- Masonry
- Plumbing
- Principles of Engineering/Technology
- Related Technical Math
- Welding
- Welding Fabrication

SkillsUSA works directly with high schools and colleges, so ask your school counselor or teacher if it is an option for you.

Skills Compétences Canada (http://skillscompetencescanada.com/en/skills-canada-national-competition). The goal of this nonprofit organization is to encourage Canadian youth to pursue careers in the skilled trades and technology sectors. Its National Competition allows young people to participate in more than forty skilled trades and technology competitions. It offers the following competitions for those interested in the trades:

- Architectural Technology & Design
- Brick Masonry
- Carpentry
- Electronics
- Electrical Installations
- Plumbing

- Refrigeration and Air Conditioning
- Sheet Metal Work
- Sprinkler Systems
- Steamfitting/Pipefitting
- Welding
- Workplace Safety

In addition to participating in the competitions, student attendees can visit a dedicated "Career Zone" that features exhibitors and participate in Try-A-Trade® and technology activities.

Text-Dependent Questions

1. How do inspectors use their technology skills?

2. What are two ways to explore construction and building inspection as a student?

3. What are SkillsUSA and Skills Compétences Canada, and what do they offer to students?

Research Project

Try at least three of the suggestions to explore the field (clubs, contests, etc.). Write a report detailing what you learned. What is the best method of exploration, and why?

■ *There is strong demand for home inspectors in the United States and in other countries.*

Words to Understand

Baby Boomer: A person who was born from the early-to-mid 1940s through 1964.

economy: Activities related to production, use, and trade of services and goods in a city, state, region, or country.

infrastructure: In relation to the construction industry, the systems of a city, region, or nation such as communication, sewage, water, transportation, bridges, dams, and electric.

radon: A naturally occurring radioactive gas that is invisible and that has no smell or taste. High radon levels can cause serious health issues—and even death.

termite: An insect that feeds on dead plants and wood. Termites can cause serious damage to homes. In fact, termites cost Americans more than $5 billion in damage each year, according to Orkin.

CHAPTER 6

The Future of the Construction and Building Inspection Occupation

The Big Picture

Construction and building inspectors play a key role in the safety of homeowners and the public. Without them, bridges might collapse, elevators would malfunction, heating and cooling systems would be installed improperly, and home buyers would

be tricked into purchasing homes that have major issues that could cost tens of thousands of dollars to fix. As a result, there will always be strong demand for inspectors.

But despite the strong need for inspectors and other trades workers, there's a shortage of skilled professionals in some countries. Globally, workers in the skilled trades were cited by employers as the most in-demand career field, according to the human resource consulting firm

■ *A housing inspector for the Federal Emergency Management Agency conducts a damage assessment after a hurricane caused extensive damage to the U.S. Virgin Islands.*

ManpowerGroup. By continent or region, skilled trades workers topped the most in-demand list in the Americas, Europe, the Middle East, and Africa. They ranked

Women in Construction and Building Inspection

Women make up about 47 percent of the U.S. workforce, but only 9 percent of construction and building inspectors. Trade unions, educational programs, construction associations, and others are trying to increase the number of women inspectors. These organizations believe that a career in inspection is a great option for women because:

- It is an interesting job that allows inspectors to make a difference in the world.

- It offers a flexible schedule for those who may not want to work a traditional schedule due to family needs or personal preferences.

- It provides an opportunity to build a business that may be especially attractive to women home buyers, who would prefer to work with other women.

Here are a few organizations that support women in the field of inspection and the construction industry:

- Women in Code Enforcement and Development (http://www.wicedicc.org) is a membership organization that offers educational seminars and training programs, a mentoring program, and networking opportunities.

- The Canadian Association of Women in Construction (http://www.cawic.ca) offers membership, a mentoring program, networking events, and a job bank at its website.

- The National Association of Home Builders (http://www.nahb.com) offers a Professional Women in Building group. Members receive *Building Women* magazine, networking opportunities, and the chance to apply for scholarships.

- The National Association of Women in Construction (NAWIC, http//www.nawic.org) offers membership, an annual meeting, and scholarships. It also publishes *The NAWIC IMAGE.*

■ *Many inspectors are nearing retirement age, which is creating many new opportunities for young people who like to identify problems at construction sites and suggest solutions.*

fourth in the Asia-Pacific region. The recruitment firm Michael Page recently conducted research to determine demand for specific careers by country. It found that there is a shortage of building inspectors in Canada and Russia.

Job opportunities for inspectors in the United States are also predicted to be good because of worker shortages and other factors. Employment for inspectors is expected to grow by 10 percent during the next decade, according to the U.S. Department of Labor (USDL). It predicts that employment will be strongest in government and in firms specializing in architectural, engineering, and related services. Inspectors who are certified, who have specialized skills, and who have experience or training in engineering, architecture, construction technology, or related areas will have better prospects than those who do not have these skills and experience. There will be many new jobs for inspectors because of the following factors:

- Many **Baby Boomer** inspectors are approaching retirement age, and there are currently not enough trainees to fill replacement needs.

- Strong job growth is occurring in the construction industry, and there is a need for construction inspectors to ensure that new factory, bridge, highway,

■ *Major efforts are being made to encourage women to pursue careers in the inspection industry.*

- About 105,000 construction and building inspectors are employed in the United States. Thirty-nine percent work for local government agencies, 16 percent for engineering services firms, 6 percent for construction companies, and 5 percent for state government agencies.

- Approximately 9 percent of construction and building inspectors are self-employed.

- About 9 percent of workers in the construction industry are women.

Source: U.S. Department of Labor

condominium, airport, pipeline, and other construction projects meet building and zoning codes. Home inspectors will be needed as the real estate market continues to bounce back after the Great Recession. (The Great Recession was a period of significant economic decline worldwide, beginning in December 2007 and ending in June 2009, in which many banks failed, the real estate sector crashed, trade declined, and many people lost their jobs.)

- Natural disasters such as tornadoes, earthquakes, hurricanes, and massive wildfires will create demand for government inspectors to examine destroyed structures to determine the amount of money that the government will reimburse property owners. Construction inspectors will be needed to examine the work of tradespeople at new home and **infrastructure** construction projects. Home inspectors will be needed to examine homes that have been damaged, and to identify areas that need repair.

- Demand is growing for inspectors who have knowledge of green construction (also known as green building), techniques that use eco-friendly or fewer construction materials (when possible), and that focus on water and energy efficiency, indoor environmental quality, and the structure's overall effects on its site or the larger community. Inspectors with expertise in rainwater harvesting systems, solar water heaters and heating systems, and other energy-efficient technology will have especially strong job prospects.

- Demand for fire inspectors will increase as states continue to integrate changes to building codes that require use of fire suppression systems.

New Technologies

In the old days, inspectors used basic tools such as screwdrivers and levels, as well as their own eyes and knowledge, to do their work. That's changed greatly in recent years—especially in the last decade. Today, inspectors still use the occasional hand tools, but also use sophisticated testing devices such as carbon monoxide analyzers, multi-meters, infrared thermometers, and moisture meters. They also use digital cameras and video recorders to document issues that they discover so that they can easily be explained to clients. Inspectors used to read unwieldly paper blueprints, but now can study them on laptops and tablet computers. Those who own contracting businesses use office management software such as Microsoft Excel and Word, customer scheduling apps, and the internet and social media (to attract and communicate with customers and coworkers). Another major technological development is the use of drones to conduct inspections of very steep roofs and other hard-to-reach areas.

These advances in technology demonstrate the need for inspectors to keep their skills up-to-date throughout their careers by taking continuing education classes offered by professional associations, government agencies, colleges, and private companies.

■ *Watch a home inspector use a drone to conduct a roof inspection.*

■ *Drones are increasingly being used by inspectors to view hard-to-reach places and get a "big-picture" view of inspection sites.*

Challenges to Employment Growth

Although inspectors will always be needed, several potential developments may limit job growth. For example, if the **economy** weakens and another recession occurs, the number of homes being sold will decline, which will slow demand for inspectors. There will also be less money available for new construction and infrastructure projects, which would reduce the number of inspectors needed to some extent.

Job opportunities may also slow if many more people enter this field after learning about job shortages. In this instance, inspectors who have specialized knowledge (green construction, energy efficiency, etc.), conduct specialized inspections (that search for mold, **radon**, or **termites**), and who are certified will have the best job prospects. If job opportunities decline, inspectors must be prepared to move to other states, or even other countries, to find work.

■ *There will be strong demand for skilled home inspectors in the next decade. Some women find this career appealing because it allows them to help others, provides a flexible schedule, and offers the opportunity to build a business and be their own bosses.*

In Closing

Can you see yourself identifying construction issues in homes and at building sites? Do you like to help others and protect the safety of the public? Do you have excellent critical-thinking and communication skills? Do you like to earn good pay without a four-year degree? If you answered "yes" to all these questions, then a rewarding career as an inspector could be in your future. I hope that you'll use this book as a starting point to discover even more about a career as a construction or home inspector. Talk to inspectors about their careers and shadow them on the job, use the resources of professional organizations and unions, and check your house out for issues such as water leaks, dry rot, low water pressure, and loose tiles to build your skills. Good luck with your career exploration!

Text-Dependent Questions

1. Can you name three reasons why employment prospects are good for inspectors?

2. How do inspectors use technology to do their jobs better?

3. What are some developments that might slow employment for inspectors?

Research Project

Inspectors increasingly need knowledge of green construction principles, and the special problems that can arise as a result of using these systems and building materials. Conduct research to learn more about green construction. Write a report about your findings and present it to your class.

Series Glossary of Key Terms

apprentice: A trainee who is enrolled in a program that prepares them to work as a skilled trades worker. Apprentices must complete 2,000 hours of on-the-job training and 144 hours of related classroom instruction during a four- to five-year course of study. They are paid a salary that increases as they obtain experience.

apprenticeship: A formal training program that often consists of 2,000 hours of on-the-job training and 144 hours of related classroom instruction per year for four to five years.

bid: A formal offer created by a contractor or trades worker that details the work that will be done, the amount the company or individual will charge, and the time frame in which the work will be completed.

blueprints: A reproduction of a technical plan for the construction of a home or other structure. Blueprints are created by licensed architects.

building codes: A series of rules established by local, state, regional, and national governments that ensure safe construction. The National Electrical Code, which was developed by the National Fire Protection Association, is an example of a building code in the United States.

building information modeling software: A computer application that uses a 3D model-based process that helps construction, architecture, and engineering professionals to more efficiently plan, design, build, and manage buildings and infra-structure.

building materials: Any naturally-occurring (clay, rocks, sand, wood, etc.) or human-made substances (steel, cement, etc.) that are used to construct buildings and other structures.

building permit: Written permission from a government entity that allows trades workers to construct, alter, or otherwise work at a construction site.

community college: A private or public two-year college that awards certificates and associate degrees.

general contractor: A licensed individual or company that accepts primary respon-sibility for work done at a construction site or in another setting.

green construction: The planning, design, construction, and operation of structures in an environmentally responsible manner. Green construction stresses energy and water efficiency, the use of eco-friendly construction materials (when possible), indoor environmental quality, and the structure's overall effects on its site or the larger community. Also known as **green building**.

inspection: The process of reviewing/examining ongoing or recently completed construction work to ensure that it has been completed per the applicable building codes. Construction and building inspectors are employed by government agencies and private companies that provide inspection services to potential purchasers of new construction or remodeled buildings.

job foreman: A journeyman (male or female) who manages a group of other journeymen and apprentices on a project.

journeyman: A trades worker who has completed an apprenticeship training. If licensed, he or she can work without direct supervision, but, for large projects, must work under permits issued to a master electrician.

Leadership in Energy and Environmental Design (LEED) certification: A third-party verification that remodeled or newly constructed buildings have met the highest criteria for water efficiency, energy efficiency, the use of eco-friendly materials and building practices, indoor environmental quality, and other criteria. LEED certification is the most popular green building rating system in the world.

master trades worker: A trades professional who has a minimum level of experience (usually at least three to four years as a licensed professional) and who has passed an examination. Master trades workers manage journeymen, trades workers, and apprentices.

prefabricated: The manufacture or fabrication of certain components of a structure (walls, electrical components, etc.) away from the construction site. Prefabricated products are brought to the construction site and joined with existing structures or components.

schematic diagram: An illustration of the components of a system that uses abstract, graphic symbols instead of realistic pictures or illustrations.

self-employment: Working for oneself as a small business owner, rather than for a corporation or other employer. Self-employed people are responsible for generating their own income, and they must provide their own fringe benefits (such as health insurance).

smart home technology: A system of interconnected devices that perform certain actions to save energy, time, and money.

technical college: A public or private college that offers two- or four-year programs in practical subjects, such as the trades, information technology, applied sciences, agriculture, and engineering.

union: An organization that seeks to gain better wages, benefits, and working conditions for its members. Also called a **labor union** or **trade union**.

zoning permit: A document issued by a government body that stipulates that the project in question meets existing zoning rules for a geographic area.

zoning rules: Restrictions established by government bodies as to what type of structure can be built in a certain area. For example, many cities have zoning rules that restrict the construction of factories in residential areas.

Index

advancement opportunities, 20
Africa, 7, 63
Alaska, 38
American Construction Inspectors Association, 41, 59
American Society of Home Inspectors, 12, 41, 51, 56, 59
Americas, 7, 63
apprenticeships, 33–35
   journeymen inspectors, 35
architects, 20
Arkansas, 38
ASHI. *See* American Society of Home Inspectors
ASHI Reporter (publication), 56
Asia-Pacific region, 7, 65
Associated Construction Contractors of New Jersey, 52
Association of Construction Inspectors, 37, 41, 59
associations, professional, 41–42, 52, 59, 64

Baby Boomers, 62, 65
bachelor's degrees, 7, 18, 20
blueprints, 10, 13, 14, 17, 33, 68
building codes, 10, 13, 51, 67
building (home) inspectors, 6–7, 11–12, 16–18, 51
   advancement opportunities, 20
   issues discovered by, 51
   specialists, 18
building information modelling software, 20, 25
Building Women (magazine), 64

California, 38
California Apprenticeship Coordinators Association, 33
cameras, 25, 52, 68
Canada, 7, 12, 41, 65
Canadian Association of Home and Property Inspectors, 37, 42, 59
Canadian Association of Women in Construction, 64
carbon monoxide analyzers, 24, 68
certifications, 37, 44
civil engineers, 20
coatings inspectors, 15
codes, building, 10, 13, 51, 67, 68
colleges, 7, 30, 31, 34, 35–37
competitions, 58–61
construction clubs, 55–56
Construction Industry Training Board, 52
construction inspectors, 11–15, 20
   advancement opportunities, 20
   duties, 13–14
   specialists, 14–15
construction managers, 6, 20
construction site tours, 52

disaster inspectors, 15, 19, 67
disaster relief payments, 15, 67
disasters, natural, 15, 67
drones, 68

earnings, 6, 38, 42–43
   highest and lowest by U.S. state, 38
   by type of employer, 42
education. *See* training
elevator inspectors, 15
employers, types of, 13, 15, 17, 39, 42, 67
employment growth, 7, 65–69
   building code changes, 68
   challenges, 69
   geographical demand, 7, 63–65
   green construction, 67
   technologies, 68
   worker shortages, 7, 63, 65
England, 52
environments, work, 7, 11, 18–19
Europe, 7, 63
ExploretheTrades.org, 6
exploring inspection as a career
   competitions, 58–61
   construction clubs, 55–56
   high school classes, 53–54
   home-improvement shows, 54
   home inspection reports, 56
   information interviews, 55
   job shadowing, 55
   publications, 56
   virtual tours, 56
   women, 64, 67

Federal Emergency Management Agency, 63
fire inspectors, 15
future of inspection as a career, 7, 63–68
   demand, 7, 63–65
   green construction, 67
   worker shortages, 7, 63, 65

Great Recession, 13, 67
green construction, 27, 37, 67

HGTV, 54
high school, 32–33, 53–54
Holmes on Homes (TV show), 54
home-improvement shows, 54
home inspection reports, 56
home inspections, 12, 15, 16, 46, 51
   issues discovered during, 51
   YouTube, 56
home inspectors. See building (home) inspectors
H.R. Inspection Services, 44

IAEI News (publication), 56
Indiana, 38
information interviews, 55
infrared thermometers, 68
infrastructure, 10, 11, 62
injuries, 21
inspections
   home, 12, 15, 16, 46, 51, 56
   purpose of, 15
inspectors
   job of, 11–12
   soft skills, 44–45, 46–47, 48, 49–52
inspector types, 11–18, 67
   building (home), 17–18
   coatings, 15
   construction, 11–15
   disaster, 15, 19, 67
   elevator, 15
   fire, 15
   journeymen, 35
   plan examiners, 14
   public works, 15
   structural, 14
International Association of Certified Home
   Inspectors, 56
International Association of Electrical Inspectors, 37,
   42, 56, 59
International Association of Plumbing and
   Mechanical Officials, 37, 42, 59
International Brotherhood of Teamsters, 41
International Code Council, 42, 59
International Union of Operating Engineers, 41

jobs
   getting, 39–42
   job boards, 40

networking, 39–40
   professional associations, 41–42
   See also future of inspection as a career
job shadowing, 45, 47, 55
journeymen inspectors, 35

labor unions. See unions
licensing, 33

ManpowerGroup, 7, 63
Michael Page (recruitment firm), 7, 65
Microsoft Excel, 68
Microsoft Word, 68
Middle East, 7, 63
middle school, 53–54
moisture meters, 68
Montana, 38
multi-meters, 68

NAESA (National Association of Elevator Safety
   Authorities) International, 37, 42, 59
National Association of Home Builders Professional
   Women in Building, 64
National Association of Women in Construction, 64
National Fire Protection Association, 37, 41, 59
natural disasters, 15, 67
Nevada, 38
New Jersey, 38

office and customer management software, 25,
   52, 68
offshoring, 7
on-the-job training, 34, 39

payments, disaster relief, 15, 67
personal traits. See soft skills
photovoltaic-powered heating systems, 48, 51
plan examiners, 14
professional associations, 41–42, 52, 59
protective gear, 22, 25
publications, 56, 64
public works inspectors, 15
purpose of inspections, 15

reports, home inspection, 56
researching inspection as a career. See exploring
inspection as a career
respirators, 22
Richards, Heidi, 44–45
Russia, 7, 65

safety, workplace, 20–22
salaries. *See* earnings
Saltzman, Reuben, 45–47
Scotland, 52
self-employment, 10, 17, 19–20, 67
sites. *See* work environments
skills, soft, 44–45, 46–47, 48, 49–52
Skills Compétences Canada, 60–61
SkillsUSA, 58–60
social media, 68
soft skills, 44–45, 46–47, 48, 49–52
software
   building information modeling, 20, 25
   office and customer management, 25, 52, 68
South Dakota, 38
Standards of Practice, 44, 46
structural inspectors, 14
Structure Tech Home Inspections, 45–46
surveyors, 18, 20

technologies, 24, 25, 51, 52, 68
   cameras, 25, 52
   carbon monoxide analyzers, 24, 68
   drones, 68
   multi-meters, 68
   photovoltaic-powered heating system, 51
   social media, 68
Tennessee, 38
terms of the trade, 26–28
The ASHI Blog, 56
The NAWIC IMAGE (publication), 64
This Old House (TV show), 51, 54
tools of the trade, 24–25
tours
   construction sites, 52
   virtual, 56
trades as a career, 6–8
trade unions. See unions
training, 7, 11–12, 30, 31–39
   apprenticeships, 33–35
   colleges, 7, 30, 31, 34, 35–37
   high school, 32–33
   on-the-job, 34, 39
traits, personal. See soft skills
types of inspectors. See inspector types

unions, 41, 55
United Kingdom, 52
United States, 7, 12, 13, 19, 33, 35, 41, 52, 65, 67

U.S. Department of Labor (USDL), 6, 19, 33, 38, 42, 65, 67

Virtual Home Inspection Tour, 56
virtual tours, 56

Wales, 52
Washington, 38
webinars, 30, 31
women, 44–45, 47, 64, 67, 70
   interview with Heidi Richards, 44–45
   organizations supporting, 64
Women in Code Enforcement and Development, 41, 59, 64
work environments, 7, 11, 18–19
workplace safety, 20–22
WorldSkills International, 60

YouTube, 56

Photo Credits

Further Reading & Internet Resources

Dykstra, Alison. *Green Construction: An Introduction to a Changing Industry.* San Francisco: Kirshner Books, 2016.

Editors of Cool Springs Press. *Black & Decker: The Complete Guide to Plumbing.* 6th ed. Minneapolis, Minn.: Cool Springs Press, 2015.

Editors of *Family Handyman. 100 Things Every Homeowner Must Know: How to Save Money, Solve Problems and Improve Your Home.* New York: Reader's Digest, 2015.

Gibilisco, Stan, and Simon Monk. *Teach Yourself Electricity and Electronics.* 6th ed. New York: McGraw-Hill Education, 2016.

Killinger, Jerry, and LaDonna Killinger. *Heating and Cooling Essentials.* 4th ed. Tinley Park, Ill.: Goodheart-Willcox, 2014.

Korn, Peter. *Woodworking Basics: Mastering the Essentials of Craftsmanship.* Newtown, Conn.: The Taunton Press, 2014.

Litchfield, Michael, and Roger C. Robinson. *The Complete Guide to Home Inspection.* Newtown, Conn.: The Taunton Press, 2015.

Internet Resources

http://www.careersinconstruction.ca/en/career/building-inspector: This website from BuildForce Canada provides information on job duties, training, and salaries for building inspectors and more than fifty other construction and trades careers.

http://www.homeinspector.org/Home-Inspection-Virtual-Tour: Visit the American Society of Home Inspectors' website to take a virtual home inspection tour.

https://www.bls.gov/ooh/construction-and-extraction/construction-and-building-inspectors.htm#tab-1: This article from the *Occupational Outlook Handbook* provides information on job duties, educational requirements, salaries, and the employment outlook for construction and building inspectors.

https://nationalcareersservice.direct.gov.uk/job-profiles/building-site-inspector: This resource from the United Kingdom's National Careers Service provides information on job duties, educational requirements, key skills, salaries, and the work environment for building site inspectors.

http://www.oldhouseweb.com/how-to-advice/a-glossary-of-home-inspection-terms.shtml: Learn the meaning of dormer, slab, parapet wall, buckling, and other home inspection terms by visiting this website from Old House Web.

About the Author

Andrew Morkes has been a writer and editor for more than 25 years. He is the author of more than 20 books about college-planning and careers, including many titles in this series, the *Vault Career Guide to Social Media*, and *They Teach That in College!?: A Resource Guide to More Than 100 Interesting College Majors*, which was selected as one of the best books of the year by the library journal *Voice of Youth Advocates*. He is also the author and publisher of "The Morkes Report: College and Career Planning Trends" blog.

Video Credits

Chapter 1: A city construction inspector discusses his career: http://x-qr.net/1Gzm

A home inspector discusses how he performs home inspections: http://x-qr.net/1HfF

Chapter 4: Learn about classroom, web simulation, and hands-on inspection training offered by the American Home Inspectors Training Institute: http://x-qr.net/1FZG

Learn some networking do's and don'ts: http://x-qr.net/1GTq

Chapter 5: View forty-seven home inspection issues in under three minutes: http://x-qr.net/1GdX

A home inspector discusses her work: http://x-qr.net/1GgU

Chapter 6: Watch a home inspector use a drone to conduct a roof inspection: http://x-qr.net/1FWM